LET'S FIND OUT! TRANSPORTATION

ALL ABOUT CARS

SARAH MACHAJEWSKI

Published in 2017 by Britannica Educational Publishing (a trademark of Encyclopædia Britannica, Inc.) in association with The Rosen Publishing Group, Inc.
29 East 21st Street, New York, NY 10010

Copyright © 2017 The Rosen Publishing Group, Inc. and Encyclopædia Britannica, Inc. Encyclopædia Britannica, Britannica, and the Thistle logo are registered trademarks of Encyclopædia Britannica, Inc. All rights reserved.

Distributed exclusively by Rosen Publishing.
To see additional Britannica Educational Publishing titles, go to rosenpublishing.com.

First Edition

Britannica Educational Publishing
J.E. Luebering: Executive Director, Core Editorial
Mary Rose McCudden: Editor, Britannica Student Encyclopedia

Rosen Publishing
Christine Poolos: Editor
Nelson Sá: Art Director
Nicole Russo: Designer
Cindy Reiman: Photography Manager
Sherri Jackson: Photo Researcher

Library of Congress Cataloging-in-Publication Data

Names: Machajewski, Sarah, author.
Title: All about cars / Sarah Machajewski.
Description: First edition. | New York : Britannica Educational Publishing, [2017] | Series: Let's find out! Transportation | Includes bibliographical references and index. | Audience: 1-4.
Identifiers: LCCN 2015047446| ISBN 9781680484403 (library bound : alk. paper) | ISBN 9781680484489 (pbk. : alk. paper) | ISBN 9781680484175 (6-pack : alk. paper)
Subjects: LCSH: Automobiles--Juvenile literature. | Automobiles--Environmental aspects--Juvenile literature.
Classification: LCC TL147 .M23 2017 | DDC 629.222--dc23
LC record available at http://lccn.loc.gov/2015047446

Photo credits: Cover, p. 1 Mino Surkala/Shutterstock.com; p. 4 Justin Sullivan/ Getty Images; p. 5 Ringo Chiu/AFP/Getty Images; p. 6 altrendo images/Stockbyte/Thinkstock; p. 7 Calvin Chan/Shutterstock.com; p. 8 Rawpixel.com/Shutterstock.com; p. 9 carroteater/Shutterstock.com; pp. 10, 11, 12, 13 Encyclopedia Britannica, Inc.; p. 14 PHAS/Universal Images Group/Getty Images; pp. 15, 19 Car Culture® Collection/Getty Images; p. 16 Keystone/Hulton Archive/Getty Images; p. 17 Heritage Images/Hulton Archive/Getty Images; p. 18 American Stock Archive/Archive Photos/Getty Images; p. 20 H. Armstrong Roberts/ClassicStock/Archive Photos/Getty Images; p. 21 Hulton Archive/Getty Images; p. 22 Library of Congress, Washington, D.C. (digital no. 3b11564); p. 23 Three Lions/Hulton Archive/Getty Images; p. 24 Keystone-France/Gamma-Keystone/Getty Images; p. 25 Frederic Lewis/Archive Photos/Getty Images; p. 26 pio3/Shutterstock.com; p. 27 Sean Gallup/Getty Images; pp. 28, 29 Bloomberg/Getty Images; interior pages background image MCCAIG/E+/Getty Images

Contents

How Do You Get Around?	4
Many Kinds of Cars	6
Under the Hood	8
Getting in Gear	10
First Attempts	14
The First True Automobiles	16
Cars Come to America	18
Henry Ford and the Model T	20
A New Era Begins	24
A Cleaner Earth	26
Cars of the Future	28
Glossary	30
For More Information	31
Index	32

How Do You Get Around?

Today, cars cover our highways. A sight like this wasn't possible just a century ago!

How do you get to school? You may walk, ride your bike, or take a bus. Your parents may drop you off in your family's car. All the ways you can get to school are forms of transportation. Cars are one of the most popular forms of transportation.

Cars are also called automobiles or motor vehicles. Trucks and buses are motor vehicles, too.

It's hard to imagine what life was like before there were

cars. That's how important they are. Cars have made it easy for people to travel within a city or across a continent. They've also affected how people live. Before, people could only work at jobs close to where they live. Now, people can live farther away from their jobs because they can drive to where they work.

> **COMPARE AND CONTRAST**
>
> Trucks, buses, motorcycles, and cars are all motor vehicles. How are they different? How are they the same?

Cars take us to school in the morning. They also take our parents to work.

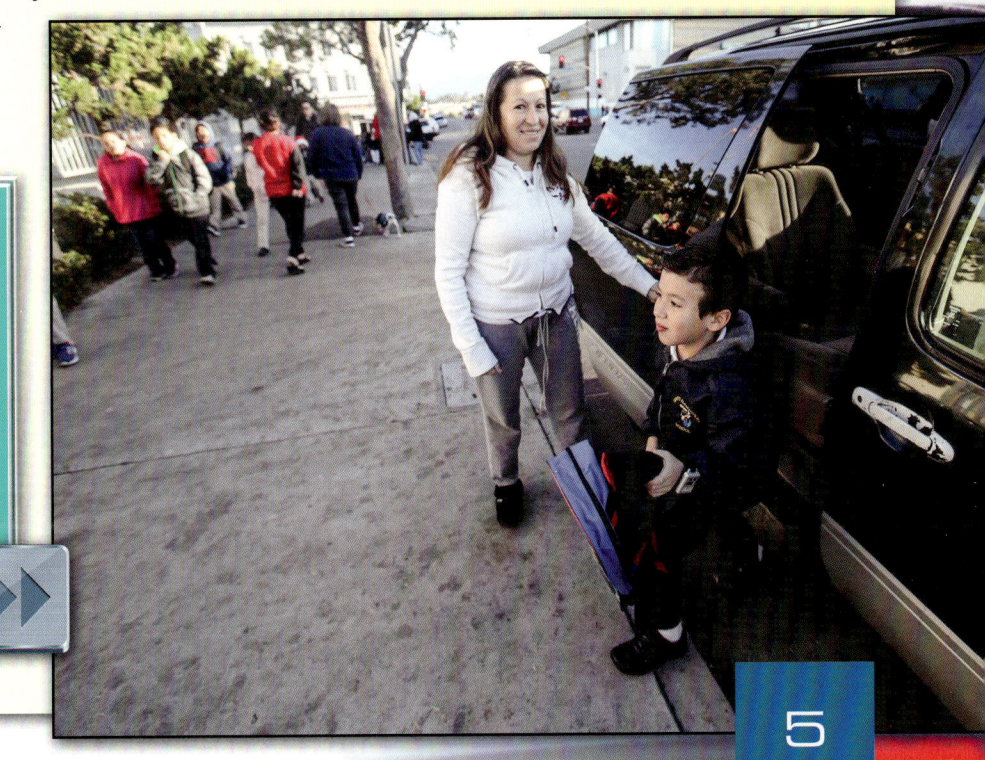

Many Kinds of Cars

What do you picture when you think of a car? There are many types of cars to choose from. In fact, the only thing the different kinds may have in common is that they all have four wheels! In the past, most cars were open, without a fixed top. Now, most cars are closed, except for a kind of car called a convertible.

The most common styles of cars are coupes and sedans. A coupe

A convertible lets you feel the sun on your face and the wind in your hair.

Racecars zoom down a racetrack. These cars are too fast for people to drive on regular roads.

An SUV is a sport utility vehicle. They are higher off the ground than sedans and often are more powerful.

has two doors and a small backseat. Sedans commonly have four doors and can seat between four and six people. When a sedan has a door in back that lifts, it's called a hatchback. Sports cars are built low to the ground and often do not have backseats. They're fast and fun! Minivans and SUVs are popular with families. They're roomy and big.

Under the Hood

All cars share the same basic parts: a body, wheels, an engine, a steering system, and brakes. The body is the outer shell. Most auto bodies are made of steel, but some are made of strong plastics or fiberglass. The body is attached to a chassis. This consists of a frame that holds all the other parts of a car together.

A hood is located at the front of the car. The engine is

A car's body is what you see first. The body is the car's outer shell.

Opening a car's hood reveals its engine. The engine may be the most important part of the car. It's what keeps the vehicle going.

usually located under the hood. (In some cars the engine is in the back of the car.) Some of the first automobiles had steam engines. Later cars were built with electric engines, but those cars couldn't reach high speeds. Electric engines were replaced by gas engines, which are commonly used today. However, some carmakers are developing electric engines again because they are better for the environment.

THINK ABOUT IT

Cars all over the world use gas engines, which create a lot of air pollution. How does this affect the environment?

Getting in Gear

A driver starts a car with a key or a button, which turns on the engine. Most cars have internal-**combustion** engines. In this kind of engine, a mix of air

Combustion is the process of burning something. In internal-combustion engines, gasoline is burned inside.

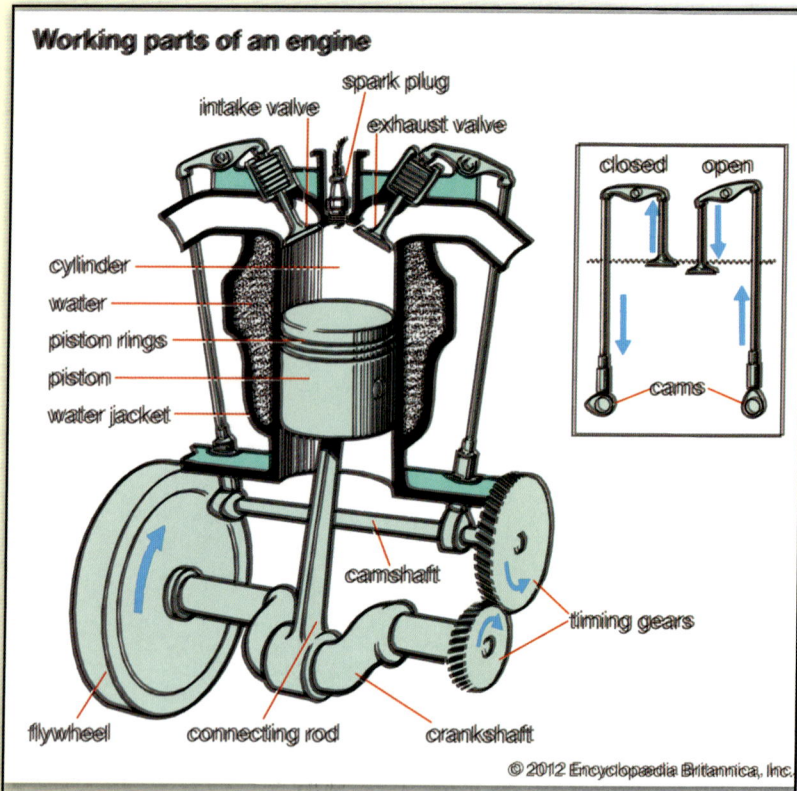

Working parts of an engine

Car engines are very complicated machines.

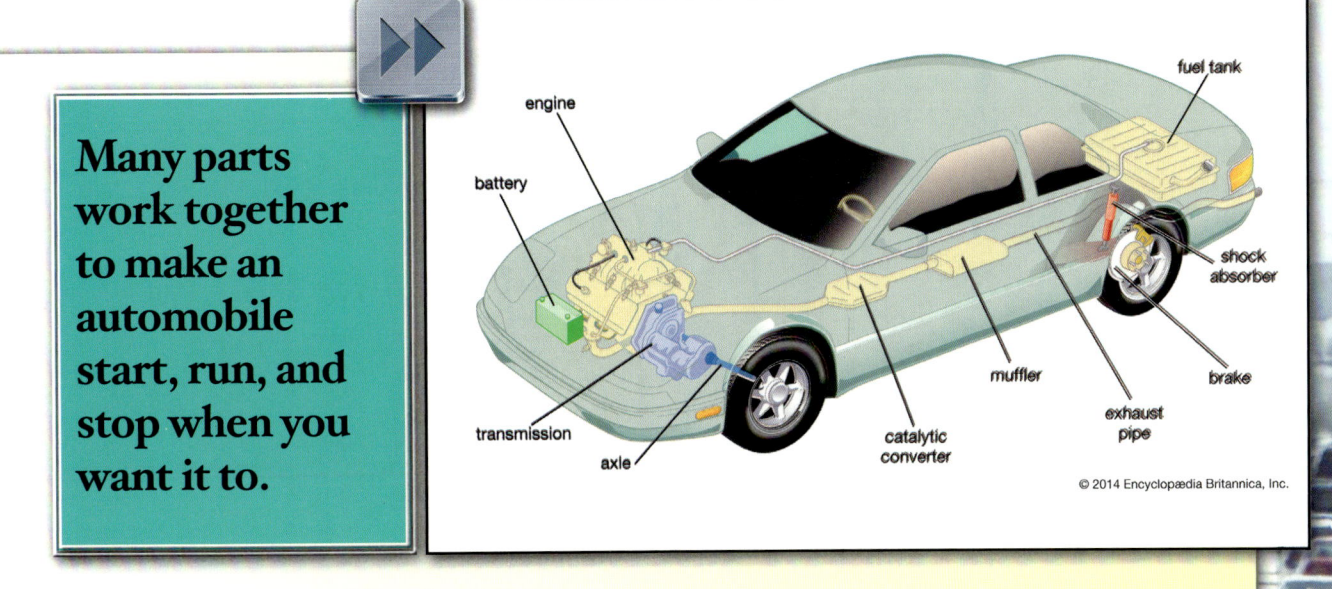

Many parts work together to make an automobile start, run, and stop when you want it to.

and fuel enters a cylinder through valves. Inside the cylinder, the mixture makes small explosions. The air-fuel mixture is ignited by spark plugs. They get their power from a battery.

Inside the cylinder, the expanding gas pushes on something called a piston. The piston goes up and down as the gas expands and contracts. Then rods convert the piston's movement into power for the car.

An exhaust system carries burned gases from the engine to the muffler. The muffler cools the gases and reduces their pressure. A car's engine gets very hot, so a cooling system helps it cool down.

POWER TRAIN

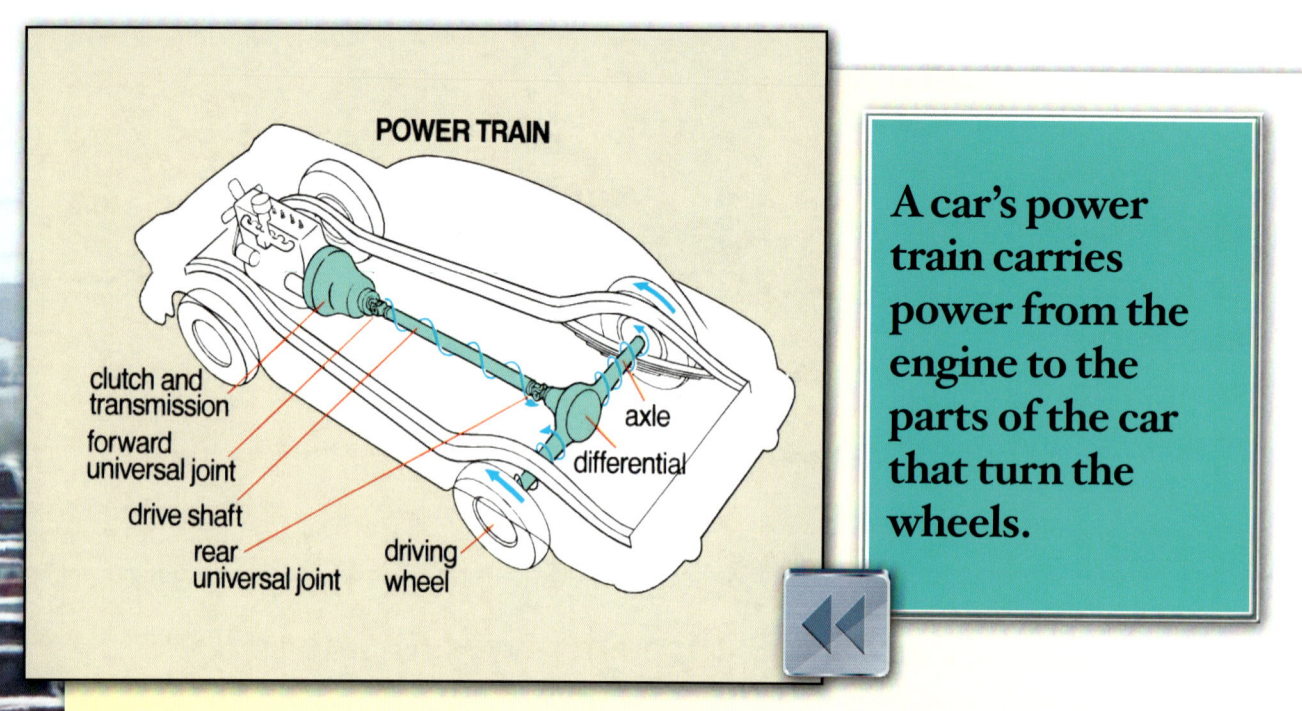

clutch and transmission
forward universal joint
drive shaft
rear universal joint
axle
differential
driving wheel

A car's power train carries power from the engine to the parts of the car that turn the wheels.

    The parts of a car that deliver power from the engine to the wheels are called the power train. The transmission is the part that controls how much speed and power the engine provides. A drive shaft carries this power from the transmission to the four wheels.

    Brake pedals control the system that brings a car to a stop. When a driver presses the brake pedal, pistons send brake fluid through pipes to the brakes. The fluid helps move a part that pushes against the wheel to make it stop. Each wheel has its own brake.

Automobile suspension and steering

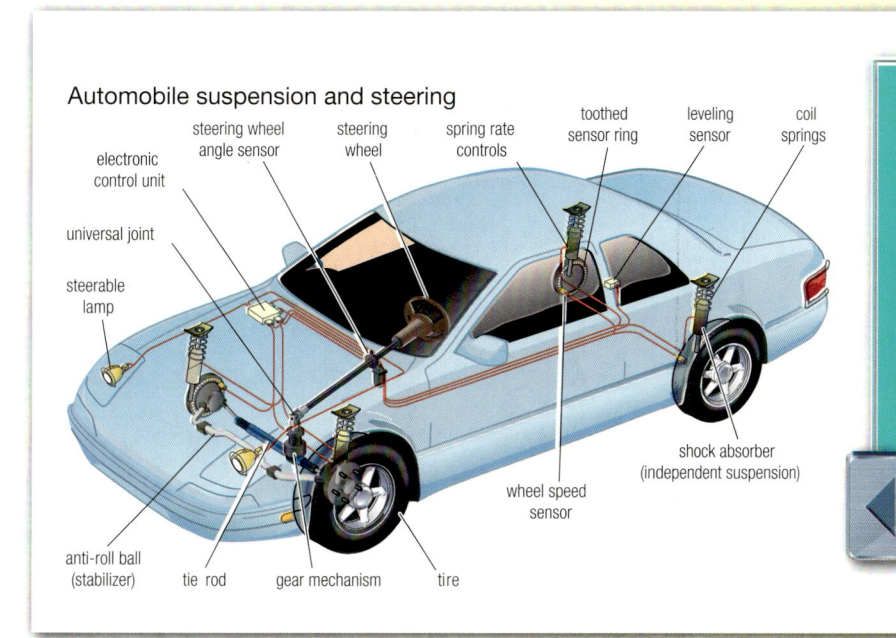

- electronic control unit
- steering wheel angle sensor
- steering wheel
- spring rate controls
- toothed sensor ring
- leveling sensor
- coil springs
- universal joint
- steerable lamp
- shock absorber (independent suspension)
- wheel speed sensor
- anti-roll ball (stabilizer)
- tie rod
- gear mechanism
- tire

A car's steering system connects the steering wheel to the parts that help the wheels turn.

Wheels are attached to a car's suspension system. A suspension system has springs that absorb bumps. Car tires are designed to keep a car from sliding on slippery or loose surfaces.

Think About It

How do the different systems work together to keep the car in motion, help it stop, and make the ride safe and comfortable for passengers?

First Attempts

In the late 1600s, inventors developed an engine that ran on steam. The steam engine changed the world. It provided power for factories, mines, and railroads. It was also used in the first car. Nicolas-Joseph Cugnot of France built the first car-like vehicle in 1769. It was powered by a steam engine and had three wheels. Many companies produced cars that used steam engines during the later 1890s and early 1900s. One problem with the steam engine was that water had to come to a boil before the car could go. During this same period, other

Early cars ran on water—boiling water! Water heated to a boil created steam, which powered the car.

companies built cars run by electric motors. Electric cars ran smoothly and were easy to operate. However, they did not run well at high speeds. Also, they could not go very far before the battery ran out and had to be recharged.

Compare and Contrast

Compare and contrast cars that used steam engines and cars that used electric engines.

The gas-powered Mercedes Benz Patent Motor Car is considered the first true automobile.

The First True Automobiles

Car technology changed with the creation of the gasoline engine. Étienne Lenoir of France developed a gas-powered internal-combustion engine in 1860. Nikolaus Otto improved upon it in 1876. Around the same time, a German man named Karl Benz was tinkering with the gas engine, too. He also invented spark plugs, gear shifters, a water radiator, a

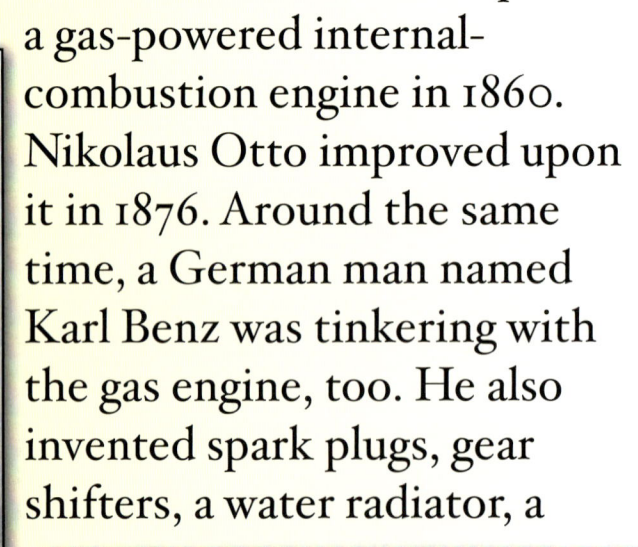

> Some people consider Karl Benz, pictured here, the father of the automobile.

> The **ignition** is the part of a car that starts the burning of fuel inside an engine.

> By 1898, cars like the one pictured here were coming off Benz's production line.

clutch, and a battery-powered **ignition** system. By 1885 Benz assembled all of these parts into what many people consider to be the first true automobile.

Benz's vehicle had a gas engine and three wheels. Benz began selling his car in 1888. That same year, Benz's wife, Bertha, and her sons took the Benz Patent Motor Car on the world's first long-distance journey by car. The Benz family's journey showed the world that cars were easy to use. By 1900 cars were a common sight on European roads.

Cars Come to America

Brothers Charles and J. Frank Duryea were in the bicycle business, but seeing a gasoline engine at the Ohio State Fair in 1886 shifted their focus. In 1891, Charles completed a design for a gas-powered, four-wheeled car. The brothers built it over two years.

On September 22, 1893, in Springfield, Massachusetts, it ran successfully for the first time.

Charles Duryea poses in his third car in this 1895 photograph.

> **THINK ABOUT IT**
>
> Cars and bicycles are two forms of transportation that developed around the same time. How did they change the way people moved from place to place?

The Duryea brothers' car was the first gas-powered automobile built and operated in America. In 1896, the Duryea Motor Wagon Company was the first car company to open in the United States. Other companies set up factories soon after.

Gas-engine cars were soon more popular than steam- and electric-powered cars. Cars became larger, faster, and easier to use. By 1910 carmakers started adding features, such as folding tops, to keep passengers out of the rain!

As cars became more popular, manufacturers added new features like collapsible tops.

Henry Ford and the Model T

At first, making cars was an expensive and slow process. Skilled craftsmen built cars from parts that were made by hand. Because of that, only wealthy people could afford to buy a car. This changed in the early 20th century thanks to a man named Henry Ford.

In 1899 Ford helped start the Detroit Automobile Company. The company focused on making cars to order for wealthy clients. He left the company and founded the Ford Motor Company in 1903.

Early cars were a luxury that could only be afforded by the very wealthy.

THINK ABOUT IT

How did making his own parts allow Ford to keep down costs?

Ford had decided he wanted to make an automobile for the general public.

At this time, automobile companies bought parts to build cars. Ford, however, wanted his company to make each and every part for its cars. He acquired iron and coal mines, forests, and mills to produce steel, fuel, wood, glass, and leather. He also bought railroad and steamship lines to transport his products easily.

Henry Ford made cars more affordable and more accessible to the masses.

THINK ABOUT IT

Before cars, most people were limited to working near their home, since travel took time and was expensive. How did cars change this?

In 1908 the Ford Motor Company began producing the Model T. This car changed the world. It was sturdy and practical. Most importantly, it was cheap to make and cheap to buy because it was mass-produced.

Mass production is making things in large numbers to keep costs down. An important part of mass production

Model Ts roll off the production line in Detroit, Michigan.

is the assembly line. In an assembly line, a product is put together one piece at a time as it moves past workers on a belt. Each worker does just one task.

Ford didn't invent the assembly line, but he perfected it. His company used it for the first time in 1913. By the 1920s, Ford's assembly lines had produced millions of Model T cars.

The Model T was much more affordable than other cars. Many people were able to buy a car for the first time.

It was often said that Ford told customers that they could have the Model T painted any color they wanted—as long as that was black.

A New Era Begins

Manufacturing means using raw materials to make products by hand or using machines.

The Ford Motor Company helped bring cars to the mass public, but several other car companies were producing cars at the same time. Many of them, including Ford, operated in Detroit, Michigan. Detroit became the automobile capital of the world in the 20th century. Today, automobile **manufacturing** is still important in the area, but cars are made all over the world.

Germany's Volkswagen Beetle was an early form of compact car.

Cars have changed greatly since they were first invented. The first cars had no covering. They had a single seat, an engine, a steering device, and three or four large wheels. By the 1940s and 1950s American cars had become very large, but now cars come in many different sizes. They also have power steering, power brakes, automatic controls for windows and seats, and air conditioning.

Modern cars also have many features to keep people safe. Seat belts, air bags, and stronger frames keep riders protected if they are in an accident.

An oil crisis in the 1970s made Americans reconsider their large cars. Small cars from Japan became popular.

A Cleaner Earth

Even though cars have had many positive effects on society, they've had a harmful effect on the environment. Cars cause widespread air pollution because gasoline produces harmful gases as it burns.

Another problem with gasoline is that it is made from oil, which is a nonrenewable resource. That means that it cannot be replaced when it is used up. In the 21st century, some automakers have tried to solve this problem by making cars that use

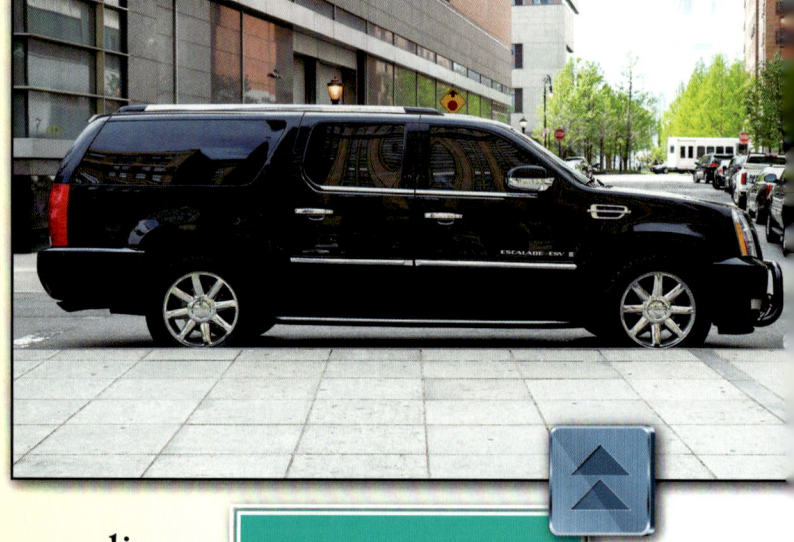

Large vehicles use more gas than small cars and add more harmful gases to the air.

Compare and Contrast

Gasoline and alternative energy sources are both used to power cars. Compare and contrast them and their effect on the environment.

alternative energy sources. An alternative energy source is an energy source that cannot be used up.

Some cars run on biofuels, such as ethanol. Ethanol is a fuel made from corn oil. Other cars run on batteries. Hybrid cars run on a combination of gas and electric power. These cars are "refueled" by plugging in at charging stations, which are located around the country.

Electric cars and charging stations may be a more common sight as time goes on.

Cars of the Future

Today's cars are different than anyone could have imagined a century ago. They have features such as **GPS** and cameras that help prevent drivers from hitting things.

Can you imagine a

"GPS" stands for "Global Positioning System." This is a tool that uses signals from satellites in the sky to help people find their way from place to place.

The car dashboards of today reflect the many innovations in technology since the first cars were invented.

> Automobile manufacturers are always improving on the car. Self-driving cars may be in our future.

car with no driver? Several car companies are currently testing self-driving cars. The cars have cameras, radar, sensors, and computers that help them speed up, brake, and stay in their lanes. The companies hope their self-driving cars will reduce accidents. They also hope that the cars will allow people who cannot drive to get around independently.

There's no telling what the future of car technology holds. Maybe one day flying cars will be more than just science fiction. For now, cars will continue to be popular so long as they continue transporting people, quickly, efficiently, and safely.

Glossary

acquire To gain.
biofuel Fuel made from plant matter or animal waste.
chassis A supporting frame, such as the body of a car.
clutch In cars, a device that connects and disconnects the wheels from the engine.
cylinder A long round hollow container. In internal-combustion engines, a part in which a piston moves up and down.
design A sketch, model, or plan.
efficient Capable of doing work without wasting time or energy.
environment Surroundings.
hybrid A mix of things.
ignite To set on fire.
nonrenewable Unable to be replaced.
pressure The force applied to something.
technology The use of science to solve a problem.

For More Information

Books

Bailey, Diane. *How the Automobile Changed History*. Edina, MN: ABDO Publishing, 2015.

Baxter, Roberta. *The First Cars*. North Mankato, MN: Capstone Press, 2014.

Gregory, Josh. *Henry Ford: Father of the Auto Industry*. New York, NY: Scholastic, 2013.

Hunter, Nick. *How Electric and Hybrid Cars Work*. New York, NY: Gareth Stevens Publishing, 2013.

Salzmann, Mary Elizabeth. *Automobile (Amazing Inventions)*. Edina, MN: ABDO Publishing, 2015.

Websites

Because of the changing nature of Internet links, Rosen Publishing has developed an online list of websites related to the subject of this book. This site is updated regularly. Please use this link to access this list:

http://www.rosenlinks.com/LFO/car

Index

air pollution, 9, 26
alternative energy source, 26–27
assembly line, 22–23

battery, 11, 15, 16–17, 27
Benz, Karl, 16, 17
brakes, 8, 25, 29
   pedals, 12

clutch, 16–17
coupes, 6–7
cylinder, 10–11

doors, 6–7
Duryea, Charles and J. Frank, 18, 19

engine, 8–9, 10–11, 12, 14, 15, 16, 17, 18, 19, 25
environment, 9, 26, 27

Ford, Henry, 20, 21, 23
Ford Motor Company, 20, 21, 22, 23, 24

gasoline, 10, 26, 27
   engine, 16, 18

hood, 8–9

Lenoir, Etienne, 16

mass production, 22–23
mines, 14, 21
minivans, 7
Model T, 22, 23
muffler, 11

Otto, Nikolaus, 16

parts of a car, 8, 12, 17, 20, 21, 22–23
piston, 11, 12
power train, 12

rods, 11

sedans, 6, 7
self-driving cars, 29
spark plugs, 11, 16–17

sports cars, 7
steering system, 8, 13, 25
suspension system, 13
SUVs, 7

technology, of cars, 16, 29
tires, 13
transmission, 12

wheels, 6, 8, 12, 13, 14, 17, 25

32

Cars have changed greatly since they were first invented. The first cars had no covering. They had a single seat, an engine, a steering device, and three or four large wheels. By the 1940s and 1950s American cars had become very large, but now cars come in many different sizes. They also have power steering, power brakes, automatic controls for windows and seats, and air conditioning.

Modern cars also have many features to keep people safe. Seat belts, air bags, and stronger frames keep riders protected if they are in an accident.

An oil crisis in the 1970s made Americans reconsider their large cars. Small cars from Japan became popular.

A Cleaner Earth

Even though cars have had many positive effects on society, they've had a harmful effect on the environment. Cars cause widespread air pollution because gasoline produces harmful gases as it burns.

Another problem with gasoline is that it is made from oil, which is a nonrenewable resource. That means that it cannot be replaced when it is used up. In the 21st century, some automakers have tried to solve this problem by making cars that use

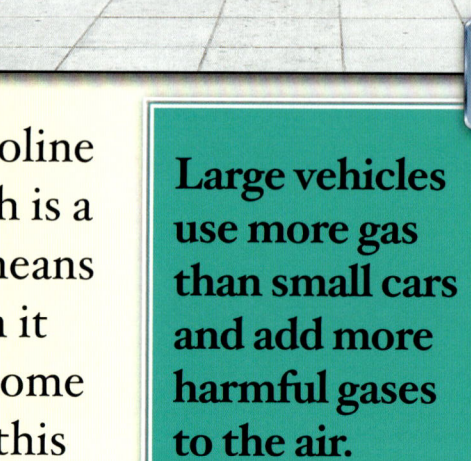

Large vehicles use more gas than small cars and add more harmful gases to the air.

> **COMPARE AND CONTRAST**
>
> Gasoline and alternative energy sources are both used to power cars. Compare and contrast them and their effect on the environment.

alternative energy sources. An alternative energy source is an energy source that cannot be used up.

Some cars run on biofuels, such as ethanol. Ethanol is a fuel made from corn oil. Other cars run on batteries. Hybrid cars run on a combination of gas and electric power. These cars are "refueled" by plugging in at charging stations, which are located around the country.

> Electric cars and charging stations may be a more common sight as time goes on.

Cars of the Future

Today's cars are different than anyone could have imagined a century ago. They have features such as **GPS** and cameras that help prevent drivers from hitting things.

Can you imagine a

"GPS" stands for "Global Positioning System." This is a tool that uses signals from satellites in the sky to help people find their way from place to place.

The car dashboards of today reflect the many innovations in technology since the first cars were invented.

> Automobile manufacturers are always improving on the car. Self-driving cars may be in our future.

car with no driver? Several car companies are currently testing self-driving cars. The cars have cameras, radar, sensors, and computers that help them speed up, brake, and stay in their lanes. The companies hope their self-driving cars will reduce accidents. They also hope that the cars will allow people who cannot drive to get around independently.

There's no telling what the future of car technology holds. Maybe one day flying cars will be more than just science fiction. For now, cars will continue to be popular so long as they continue transporting people, quickly, efficiently, and safely.

Glossary

acquire To gain.
biofuel Fuel made from plant matter or animal waste.
chassis A supporting frame, such as the body of a car.
clutch In cars, a device that connects and disconnects the wheels from the engine.
cylinder A long round hollow container. In internal-combustion engines, a part in which a piston moves up and down.
design A sketch, model, or plan.
efficient Capable of doing work without wasting time or energy.
environment Surroundings.
hybrid A mix of things.
ignite To set on fire.
nonrenewable Unable to be replaced.
pressure The force applied to something.
technology The use of science to solve a problem.

For More Information

Books

Bailey, Diane. *How the Automobile Changed History*. Edina, MN: ABDO Publishing, 2015.

Baxter, Roberta. *The First Cars*. North Mankato, MN: Capstone Press, 2014.

Gregory, Josh. *Henry Ford: Father of the Auto Industry*. New York, NY: Scholastic, 2013.

Hunter, Nick. *How Electric and Hybrid Cars Work*. New York, NY: Gareth Stevens Publishing, 2013.

Salzmann, Mary Elizabeth. *Automobile (Amazing Inventions)*. Edina, MN: ABDO Publishing, 2015.

Websites

Because of the changing nature of Internet links, Rosen Publishing has developed an online list of websites related to the subject of this book. This site is updated regularly. Please use this link to access this list:

http://www.rosenlinks.com/LFO/car

Index

air pollution, 9, 26
alternative energy source, 26–27
assembly line, 22–23

battery, 11, 15, 16–17, 27
Benz, Karl, 16, 17
brakes, 8, 25, 29
  pedals, 12

clutch, 16–17
coupes, 6–7
cylinder, 10–11

doors, 6–7
Duryea, Charles and J. Frank, 18, 19

engine, 8–9, 10–11, 12, 14, 15, 16, 17, 18, 19, 25
environment, 9, 26, 27

Ford, Henry, 20, 21, 23
Ford Motor Company, 20, 21, 22, 23, 24

gasoline, 10, 26, 27
  engine, 16, 18

hood, 8–9

Lenoir, Etienne, 16

mass production, 22–23
mines, 14, 21
minivans, 7
Model T, 22, 23
muffler, 11

Otto, Nikolaus, 16

parts of a car, 8, 12, 17, 20, 21, 22–23
piston, 11, 12
power train, 12

rods, 11

sedans, 6, 7
self-driving cars, 29
spark plugs, 11, 16–17

sports cars, 7
steering system, 8, 13, 25
suspension system, 13
SUVs, 7

technology, of cars, 16, 29
tires, 13
transmission, 12

wheels, 6, 8, 12, 13, 14, 17, 25

32